LEWISHAM AND CATFORD TRAMWAYS

Robert J Harle

D0507766

MP Middleton Press

First published February 1994

ISBN 1 873793 26 X

© Middleton Press 1994

Design - Deborah Goodridge

Published by Middleton Press
                    Easebourne Lane
                    Midhurst
                    West Sussex
                    GU29 9AZ
                    Tel: (0730) 813169
(From 16 April 1995 - (01730) 813169)

Printed & bound by Biddles Ltd,
                    Guildford and Kings Lynn

CONTENTS

Extract from London Transport Tramways map 1933.

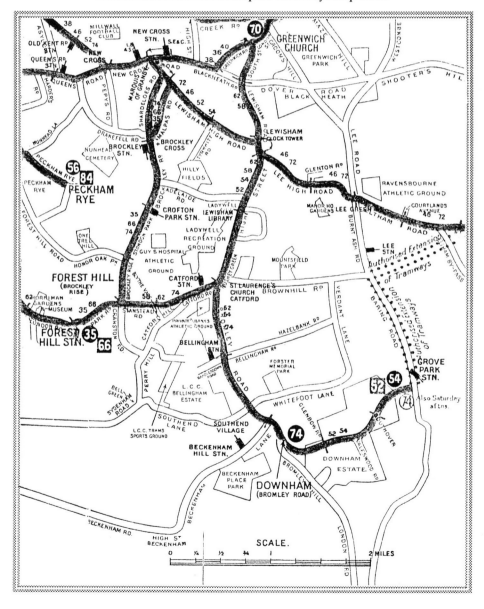

INTRODUCTION AND ACKNOWLEDGEMENTS

This third London volume in the Tramway Classics series covers most of the area of the former Metropolitan Boroughs of Deptford and Lewisham. I am again indebted to all the following photographers: C.Carter, J.C.Gillham, G.L.Gundry, J.H.Meredith, J.H.Price, D.A.Thompson, and R.J.S. Wiseman. They preserved a way of life in an urban scene which has now disappeared. My thanks also to S.E.Letts for preparing valuable photographs for publication and to D.Jones of the LCC Tramways Trust for the loan of several views. The library staff of the National Tramway Museum, Rosy Thacker and Glynn Wilton have been very helpful in supplying archive material and copies of tramway maps produced by F.Merton Atkins. G. Croughton has kindly supplied copies of tickets.

I hope this book conjures up some of the sights and sounds of a past before the motor car, motorways and housing redevelopment changed the face of South East London. Several generations have now grown up since the demise of the trams and for them this book is not about nostalgia. They will see pictures of people going about their daily lives in an age far removed from the present; the local history portrayed in this book may seem more relevant to ordinary folk than the great events of state. There are many lessons to learned from the past and a hope for the future of London must lie in the rebuilding of efficient public transport with a role for modern tramways. As I write these notes, it has been confirmed that the Docklands Light Railway will be extended to Lewisham; this will be a welcome addition to help solve traffic congestion.

GEOGRAPHICAL SETTING

The landscape of this part of London is one of hills dissected by the valleys of the Rivers Ravensbourne and Quaggy. It has been for a long time an urban landscape with the odd patch of green preserved in the form of parks or sports grounds.

All maps in this volume are to the scale of 25" to 1 mile, unless otherwise stated.

ROUTE 54   **Grove Park - Lewisham - Camberwell - Kennington - Victoria**   P.M. times ar in heavy figure

Via Downham Way, Bromley Road, Rushey Green, Lewisham High Street, Loampit Vale, Loampit Hill, Lewisham Way, New Cross Road, Queens Road, Peckham High Street, Peckham Road, Camberwell Church Street, Camberwell New Road, Harleyford Road, Vauxhall Bridge, Vauxhall Bridge Road.

RAILWAY STATIONS SERVED : Grove Park Bellingham, Lewisham, St. Johns, New Cross Gate, Queens Road *Peckham*, Oval, Vauxhall, Victoria

Service interval : WEEKDAYS 3-4 minutes, SUNDAY morning 6 minutes, afternoon and evening 4 minutes

	WEEKDAYS First		MON.–FRI. Last	SAT. Last	SUNDAY First	SUNDAY Last
GROVE PARK *Baring Road*		4 50	10 28 11 48	10 28 11 49	8 2	10 33 11 51
Downham Way *Change Pit*		4 56	10 35 11 55	10 35 11 56	5 32 8 8	10 40 11 58
Catford *St. Laurence Church*		5 4	10 43 12 3	10 43 12 4	5 40 8 16	10 48 12 6
Lewisham *Clock Tower*		5 11	10 51 12 11	10 51 12 12	5 47 8 23	10 55 12 13
New Cross Gate	4 43 4 53 5 20		11 1 12 21	11 1 12 22	5 56 8 32	11 4 12 22
Camberwell Green	4 54 5 4 5 31		11 12	11 13	6 7 8 43	11 15
Kennington Gate	5 0 5 10 5 37		11 18	11 19	6 12 8 48	11 20
Vauxhall Bridge *Bridgefoot*	5 3 5 13 5 40		11 21	11 22	6 15 8 51	11 23
VICTORIA *Clock Tower*	5 10 5 20 5 47		11 28	11 30	6 20 8 56	11 29
VICTORIA *Clock Tower*	5 15 5 25	5 53	10 46 11 30	10 45 11 31	6 26 7 7	10 51 11 31
Vauxhall Bridge *Bridgefoot*	5 22 5 32	6 0	10 53 11 37	10 52 11 38	6 31 7 12	10 57 11 37
Kennington Gate	5 25 5 35	6 3	10 56 11 40	10 55 11 41	6 34 7 15	11 0 11 40
Camberwell Green	5 31 5 41 5 58 6 9		11 2 11 46	11 2 11 48	6 39 7 20	11 5 11 45
New Cross Gate	4 16 5 42 5 52 6 9 6 20		11 13 11 57	11 14 12 0	4 24 5 7 6 50 7 31	11 16 11 56
Lewisham *Clock Tower*	4 26 5 52 6 2 6 19 6 30		11 23	11 24	4 33 5 16 6 59 7 40	11 25
Catford *St. Laurence Church*	4 34 6 0 6 10 6 27 6 38		11 31	11 32	4 40 5 23 7 6 7 47	11 32
Downham Way *Change Pit*	4 42 6 8 6 18 6 35 6 46		11 39	11 40	4 48 5 31 7 14 7 55	11 40
GROVE PARK *Baring Road*	4 48 6 15 6 25 6 42 6 53		11 46	11 47	3 1	11 47

SPECIAL EARLY JOURNEYS

Blackwall Tunnel to Downham Way, SUNDAY at 5 22 a.m., Downham Way to Blackwall Tunnel, SUNDAY at 4 4 a.m.

*–Special early journey.
†–1 minute earlier on Saturday.

HISTORICAL BACKGROUND

Deptford, now contained in the Borough of Lewisham, grew up on the banks of the Thames and it was here in 1513 that Henry VIII founded a royal dockyard. The isolated villages of Lewisham and Rushey Green, Catford did not expand greatly until the coming of better transport facilities provided by the railway companies; they built lines in the area from the 1840s onwards. Henceforth, commuting to work in the capital became the norm for thousands and this remains so today. The other form of rail transport, the horse tramway first appeared in October 1870 on a line from Blackheath Road to New Cross and this form of traction was subsequently extended along the Old Kent Road and towards Peckham. The centre of Lewisham had to wait until October 1890 for its trams when the Greenwich to Rushey Green service opened.

The progressive LCC was committed to replacing the horse with electric traction and a large programme of new tramways was started with the opening of lines through New Cross in 1904. The project gained momentum. Lewisham was reached by electric trams in 1906; Lee Green was connected to the network in the following year. The section from Greenwich to Lewisham Obelisk opened in April 1908. New Cross to Forest Hill via Brockley commenced operations in 1911 and these tracks were linked with the Dulwich services in 1915. A direct line from Brockley Rise to Rushey Green was constructed in 1913. The attention of the LCC then turned southwards and the line from Rushey Green pushed onwards to Southend Village in 1914 and was further extended after World War I to reach Valeswood Road in 1926. This tramway formed part of the new transport arrangements for the LCC Downham housing estate, and it included a conduit to trolley change pit at the beginning of Downham Way. In November 1928 the tracks finally reached Grove Park where a terminus was established pending a link up with the Eltham lines along Westhorne Avenue.

In July 1933 the London Passenger Transport Board took over. The policy of the new owners towards tramways was very different to that pursued by the London County Council. The authorised extension from Grove Park to Eltham was an early casualty of the bus and trolleybus minded Board. Tramway abandonment got going in the mid 1930s and after a brief respite for World War II it resumed in 1950. The Lewisham services were converted to buses in four stages from October 1951, and London's last tramcar entered New Cross depot in the early hours of 6th July 1952. A cheap, efficient, frequent and pollution free public service was removed from streets which became progressively more congested and fume ridden.

ROUTE 52 — **Grove Park - Lewisham - New Cross - City Southwark** — P.M. times are in heavy figures

Via Downham Way, Bromley Road, Rushey Green, Lewisham High Street, Loampit Vale, Loampit Hill, Lewisham Way, New Cross Road, Old Kent Road, Great Dover Street, Marshalsea Road, Southwark Bridge Road, Southwark Bridge.

RAILWAY STATIONS SERVED: Grove Park, Bellingham, Lewisham, St. Johns, New Cross Gate, Borough

Service interval: MONDAY to FRIDAY peak hours 6 minutes, SATURDAY morning peak hours 8 minutes, afternoon peak hours 6 minutes.

	WEEKDAYS Morning			MON. to FRI. Afternoon		SATURDAY Afternoon	
	First	Last MF	SO	First	Last	First	Last
GROVE PARK *Baring Road*	5 43	8 41 / 8 47	8 49	.. 4 30	6 6,7 54	.. 11 46	1 4 2 58
Catford *St. Laurence Church*	5 58	8 56 / 9 2	9 4	.. 4 45	6 21 8 9	.... 12 1	1 19 3 13
Lewisham *Clock Tower*	6 6	9 4 / 9 10	9 12	.. 4 53	6 29 8 17	.... 12 9	1 27 3 21
New Cross Gate	6 16	9 14 / 9 20	9 22	4 10 5 3	6 39 8 27	11 37 12 19	1 37 3 31
Old Kent Road *Bricklayers Arms*	6 27	9 25		4 21 5 14	6 50	11 48 12 30	1 48
CITY *Southwark*	6 37	9 35		4 31 5 24	7 0	11 58 12 40	1 58

	WEEKDAYS Morning	MF	SO		MON. to FRI. Afternoon		SATURDAY Afternoon	
	First				First	Last	First	Last
CITY *Southwark*	.... 6 39	7 51	7 53	9 37	.... 4 32	6 56 7 2	.... 12 0	2 0
Old Kent Road *Bricklayers Arms*	.. 6 49	8 1	8 3	9 47	.. 4 42	7 6 7 12	.... 12 10	2 10
New Cross Gate	5 8 7 0	8 12	8 14	9 58	3 55 4 53	7 17,7 23	11 9 12 21	2 21
Lewisham *Clock Tower*	5 18 7 10	8 22	8 24		4 5 5 3	7 27	11 19 12 31	2 31
Catford *St. Laurence Church*	5 26 7 18	8 30	8 32		4 13 5 11	7 35	11 27 12 39	2 39
GROVE PARK *Baring Road*	5 41 7 33	8 45	8 47		4 28 5 26	7 50	11 42 12 54	2 54

MF—Monday to Friday only. **SO—Saturday only.**

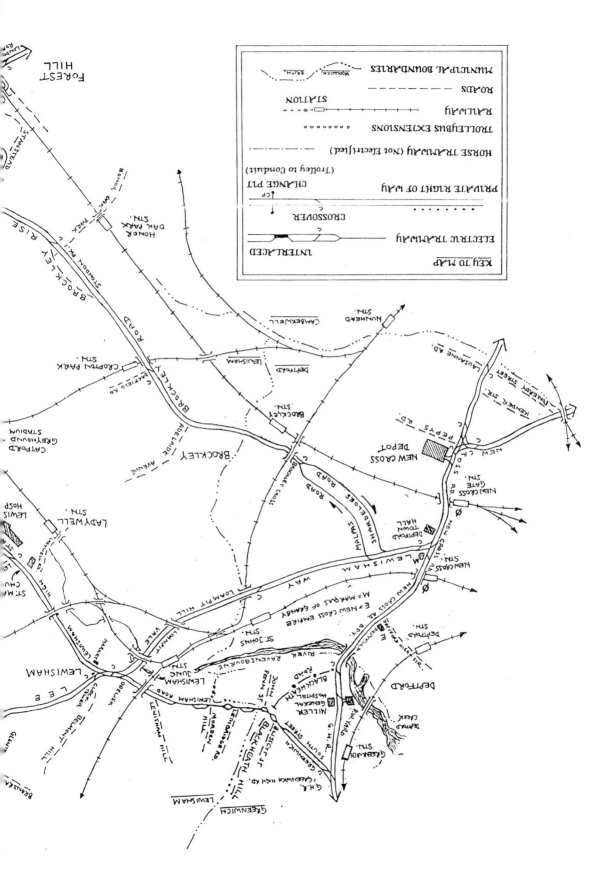

TROLLEY

CONDUIT

ROAD LEE GREEN

C BURNT ASH ROAD

BARING ROAD

GROVE PARK STN.

GROVE PARK

PARK

HITHER GRN. STN.

C

DOWNHAM WAY

LONDON
LEWISHAM

NORTHOVER

KENT
BROMLEY

C SOUTHOVER

HITHER
GREEN

RUSHEY GREEN

BROWNHILL ROAD

CATFORD

WAY

SHROFFOLD RD.

C WELLWOOD ROAD

HIPPODROME

HEY
REEN

C

HORSE TRAM DEPOT

LTH.

BROMLEY

ROAD

BELLINGHAM

BELLINGHAM ROAD

WHITEFOOT LANE

CP TROLLEY

D O W N H A M

C

CONDUIT

CB

CATFORD RD.

L.T.H
= LEWISHAM TOWN
HALL

CB = CATFORD BRIDGE
STN.

RD.
TN.

CATFORD BUS GARAGE
(TL)

C

C ROAD SOUTHEND

BROMLEY

ROAD

C

CATFORD HILL

16

B= BEECHFIELD RD.

BELLINGHAM
STN.

SOUTHEND LANE

BECKENHAM HILL ROAD

BECKENHAM
HILL STN.

ROAD

C

18

SOUTHEND LANE

½ MILE

RD.

R = WALDRAM PK. RD.
= WALDRAM PLACE
= PERRY VALE

1. New Cross Gate to Deptford

1. In the month of September 1951 car 1812 heads along New Cross Road whilst a sister car disappears in the gloom of the railway bridge in the direction of the Old Kent Road.

(R.J.S.Wiseman)

2. The sunshine returns to New Cross Gate with an Abbey Wood bound tram the sole occupant of this street scene. Car 92 was once part of the fleet operated by East Ham Corporation and it had migrated south when the tramways in that part of metropolitan Essex were converted to trolleybus operation.

(D.A.Thompson)

3. The first decade of the twentieth century saw plenty of tramway activity as this gathering of LCC cars proves. The triangular junction plays host to a number of services all observed by a small lad perched on a fruit box, perhaps the pointsman standing in the roadway was his dad. (R.J.Harley Coll.)

ROUTE 66	Forest Hill - New Cross - Kennington - Victoria	P.M. times are in heavy figures

Via Park Road Stanstead Road, Brockley Rise, Stondon Park, Brockley Road, Shardeloes Road (return via Malpas Road), Lewisham Way, New Cross Road, Queens Road, Peckham High Street, Peckham Road, Camberwell Church Street, Camberwell New Road, Harleyford Road, Vauxhall Bridge, Vauxhall Bridge Road.

RAILWAY STATIONS SERVED: Forest Hill, Crofton Park, Brockley, New Cross Gate, Queens Road *Peckham*, Oval, Vauxhall, Victoria

Service interval: MON. to FRI. 6 mins. (aft. and eve. 6-8 mins.); SAT. 8 mins. (aft. 6 mins.)

	W'KDYS First	MON. to FRI. Last	SAT. Last				W'KDYS First	MON-FRI Last	SAT Last
FOREST HILL *Station*	5 30	10 40	11 36	....	10 40	11 38	....	VICTORIA *Clock Tower*....	.... 6 18	10 48	11 28	10 48	11 30
New Cross Gate	5 49	10 59	11 55	..	10 59	11 57	..	Vauxhall *Bridgefoot*	.. 6 25	10 55	11 35	10 55	11 37
Camberwell Green	6 0	11 10	..	....	11 11	....	Kennington Gate	.... 6 28	10 58	11 38	10 58	11 40
Kennington Gate	6 6	11 16	..	..	11 18	..	..	Camberwell Green	4 14 6 34	11 4	11 44	11 5	11 47
Vauxhall *Bridgefoot*	6 9	11 19	....	....	11 21	....	..	New Cross Gate	4 25 6 45	11 15	11 55	11 17	11 59
VICTORIA *Clock Tower*	6 16	11 26	..	..	11 28	....	..	FOREST HILL *Station* ..	4 44 7 4	11 34	..	11 36	..

ADDITIONAL JOURNEYS

EARLY JOURNEYS—WEEKDAYS

Cranston Road to Savoy Street, via Blackfriars at 4 4 a.m.
Forest Hill to Blackfriars at 4 49, 5 10 a.m.
New Cross to Savoy Street, via Blackfriars at 4 11 a.m.
New Cross to Blackfriars at 5 19, 5 39 a.m.
New Cross to Camberwell at 3 21, 4 1, 4 24, 4 44 a.m.
New Cross to Cranston Road, MON. to FRI. at 5 32, 5 43 a.m.
Camberwell to Cranston Road at 3 34, a.m.
Savoy Street to Forest Hill at 4 45, 4 55 a.m.
Blackfriars to Forest Hill at 5 38, 5 50, 6 1, 6 10 a.m.

LATE JOURNEYS—MONDAY to FRIDAY

New Cross to Camberwell at 12 54 a.m.
Forest Hill to Savoy Street, via Blackfriars at 11 25 p.m.
Savoy Street to New Cross, via Blackfriars at 12 20 a.m.
Camberwell to New Cross at 1 7 a.m.

LATE JOURNEYS—SUNDAY

New Cross to Savoy Street, via Blackfriars at 11 44 p.m.
New Cross to Camberwell at 12 54 a.m.
Savoy Street to New Cross, via Blackfriars at 12 20 a.m.
Camberwell to New Cross at 1 7 a.m.

4. Protest marches are nothing new, and as the fluttering banners pass by, one wonders what the interested spectators on the top deck were thinking. The date is 18th May 1907 and the Woolwich Arsenal workers were en route to Westminster to lobby Parliament. (J.H.Price Coll.)

5. Car 2 still looks fit for another thirty years service, but alas this is the last day, 5th July 1952 and tomorrow she will be residing in the scrap yard at Penhall Road, Charlton. The expendible nature of public transport is further illustrated behind the tram by an ex-Midland Red bus HA 5062 on tow to a final resting place. (John H.Meredith)

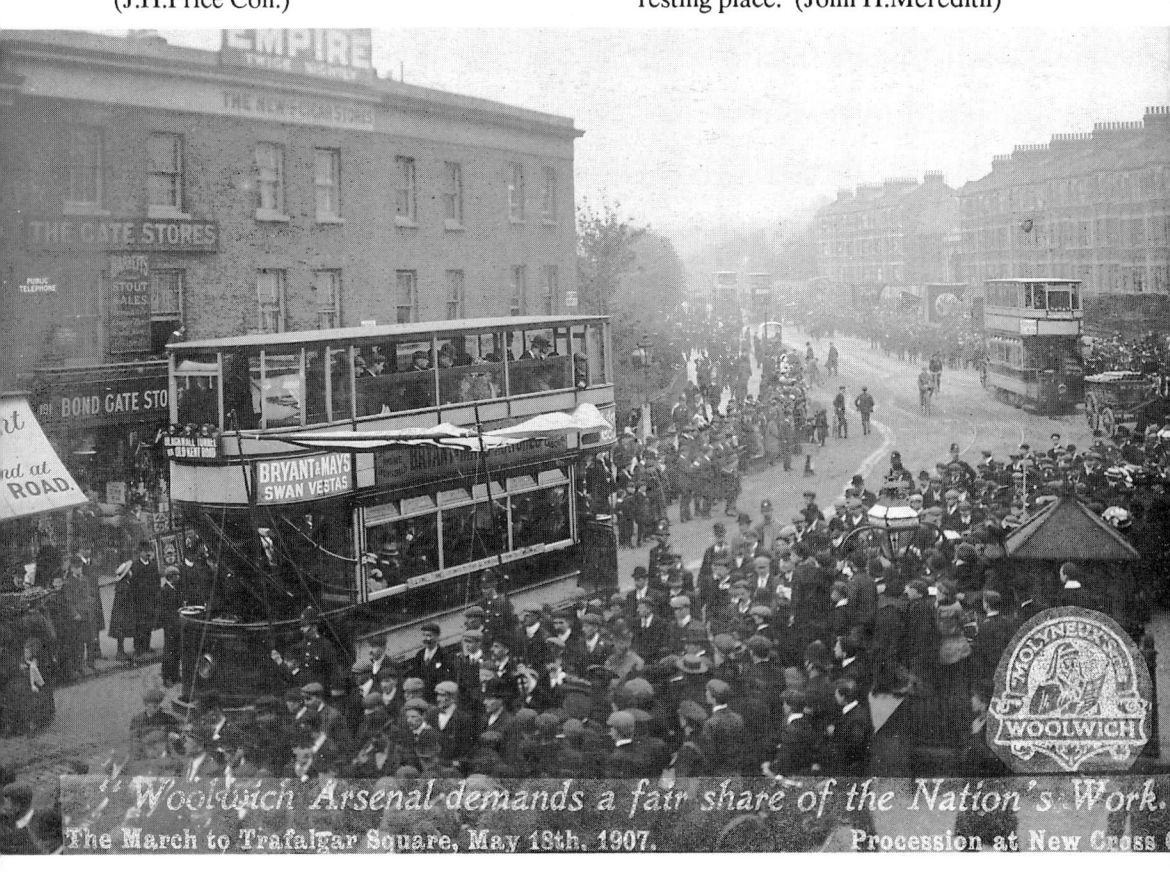

Woolwich Arsenal demands a fair share of the Nation's Work.
The March to Trafalgar Square, May 18th, 1907. Procession at New Cross

6. We pull back slightly from the junction in this 1920s panorama to observe the variety of public transport on display, with some complimentary pedal power in the foreground. (R.J.Harley Coll.)

7. During the tramway era the lines of trams waiting outside New Cross depot were a famous local sight. Cars would be taken in and out of service, whilst replacement crew members stood about on the pavement. (R.J.S.Wiseman)

8. Rain sweeps down as car 2072 heads from Telford Avenue depot to Penhall Road where it will await collection for the journey to Leeds. Many of these Feltham type trams survived in the Yorkshire city until 1959. The peak traffic flow past this spot outside the depot was 225 trams per hour! (John H.Meredith)

9. Almost half a century earlier than the previous view, LCC car 68 heads for Woolwich Road whilst car 75 is about to reverse for the return to Southwark Bridge, which was the nearest tramway terminus to the City of London. The City "establishment" had always made it quite clear that it wanted nothing to do with tramways, even going so far as to maintain that the LCC tramcars would encourage the "great unwashed" to pollute the fair streets between St.Pauls and the Bank. (R.J.Harley Coll.)

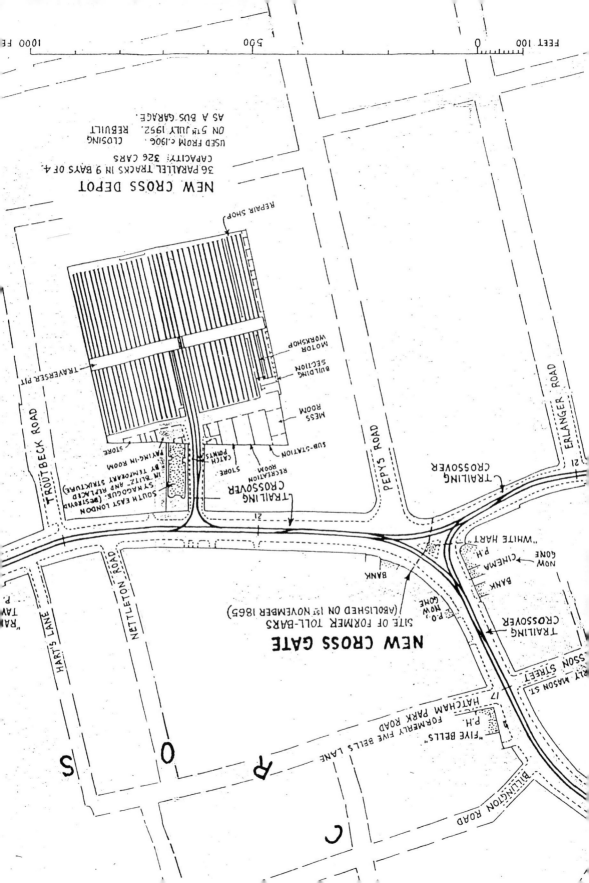

10. This view of the Portland stone, Roman-Doric style entrance to New Cross depot gives no indication of the sheer size of the building. On its completion in 1905 New Cross car shed had a capacity of 314 bogie cars or 350 single truck cars, which were shorter than the eight wheelers. (R.J.Harley Coll.)

11. This 1933 picture was taken to feature the experimental pantograph on car 1172 which is also illustrated in picture no. 80. It was claimed that the depot was the largest building of its type in Great Britain. (LCC Official Photo)

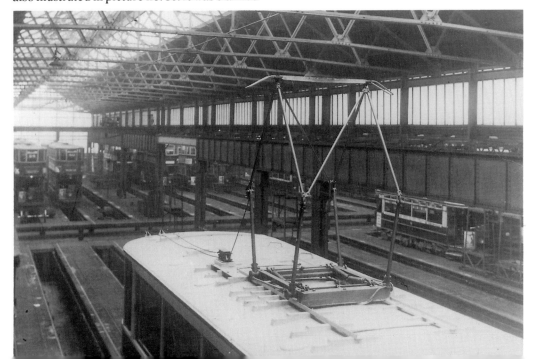

12. On the slope leading to New Cross Road, one can imagine the dialogue between the small boys and the motorman ...'Ere, Mister, 'ow much is that tram?.... Five bob to you sonny, but you'll have to take it yourself, 'cos next week we start ripping up the rails!...The reader may have noticed that the smart stone entrance way is missing, this was demolished by that well known German vandal, A.Hitler. (R.J.S.Wiseman)

14. Horse drawn vehicles mingle with LCC car 211 in an Edwardian view of Deptford Town Hall. This fine building is embellished by a number of motifs of a nautical flavour, reflecting the borough's links with Thames shipping. (R.J.Harley Coll.)

13. The man with the red flag is controlling the traffic as he waves on an approaching tramcar out of shot in the depot entrance. (R.J.S.Wiseman)

15. The parting of the ways at the Marquis of Granby. Car 1871 sways gracefully in a Woolwich direction whilst East Kent Leyland CFN 102 faces a journey along the A20 to the Channel coast. (John H.Meredith)

16. It is amazing how little traffic was about on this fine summer's day as a service 36 tram makes its stately way past New Cross SR and Underground stations. In an age before yellow lines even the No Waiting signs seem superfluous. (D.A.Thompson)

S.E.R. Station, New Cross Rd

17. The expressions of many of the bystanders seem to reflect the hope and confidence of a new century. The LCC trams had taken a lot of traffic away from the suburban railways. Slow steam trains were no match for the latest electric marvels running along the street close to everybody's front door. (G.L.Gundry Coll.)

18. Plenty of activity in Deptford Broadway. The driver of car 333 which has just crossed Deptford Bridge edges past the brass band. One gets the feeling that wearing a hat was compulsory in the early 1900s. (R.J.Harley Coll.)

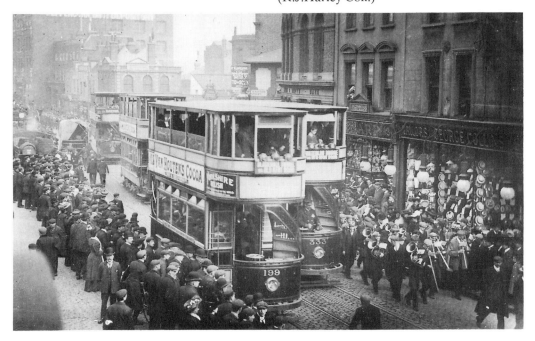

19. Car 186 precedes a convoy of period road haulage vehicles. South London Motorcycles on the corner of Greenwich High Road would no doubt be selling AJS, Norton, Matchless etc., some of the splendid British names of the past. (D.A.Thompson)

20. A cyclist passes the entrance to Miller General Hospital as a service 38 car draws up to the stop outside the offices of Merryweathers, famous for their fire engines and at one time, builders of steam tram locos. The lady on the left of the picture is walking by the gate of the Deptford PW yard. (D.A.Thompson)

21. On the platform of car 594 two ladies are chatting, no doubt they are having to speak up as the tram clatters over the points to Deptford yard. A posse of cyclists races in the other direction. The eagle-eyed tramway expert will have spotted that the tram is on a depot run to take up service at Greenwich Church, normally service 70 did not run along this road. (John H.Meredith)

22. Deptford Permanent Way yard was the setting for an amazing collection of vehicles and machinery dedicated to the maintenance of the tramway system. An unusual visitor is car 1400 which is standing next to the weigh bridge. (John H.Meredith)

23. There was a horse tramway pedigree to the Deptford yard and the antique air is further enhanced by these two marvellous Albion lorries, BXO 894 and its sister BXO 895. You needed a strong right arm to hand crank the engine on a cold winter's morning! (John C.Gillham)

24. The LCC used the wharf on Deptford Creek to unload materials from barges, in this way London Transport inherited the tramway steam crane seen here. Other crane jibs echo the shape of the Skylon at the 1951 Festival of Britain. (John C.Gillham)

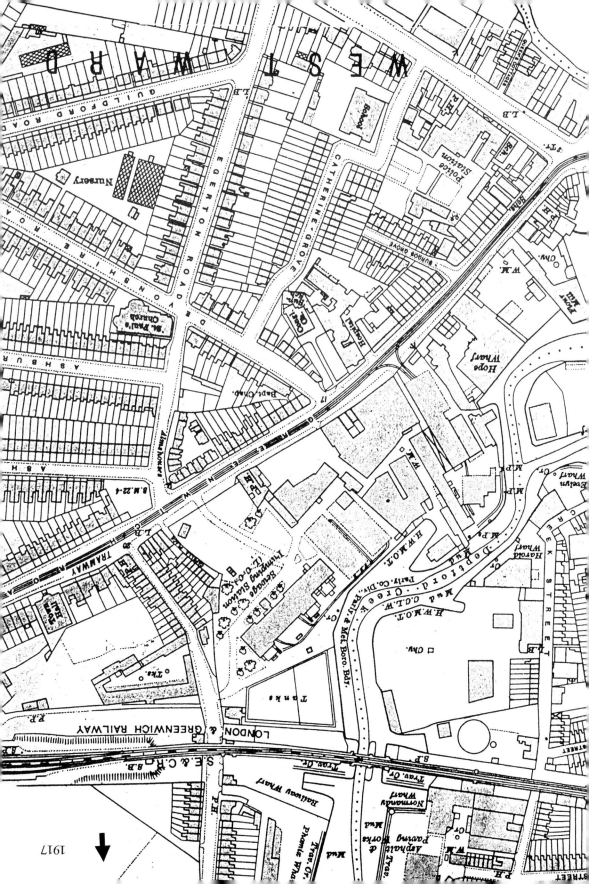

2. New Cross to Lewisham

25. A dignified procession enters Lewisham Way. In this June 1951 photograph the motorman of car 122 must be looking forward to reaching the terminus at Forest Hill. He had already driven all the way from Highgate in North London via the famous Kingsway Subway. (R.J.S.Wiseman)

26. At the crossing of Lewisham Way with Amersham Road and Shardeloes Road, car 1087 negotiates the points where the "up" line from Brockley joins carrying services 35, 66 and 74. (John H.Meredith)

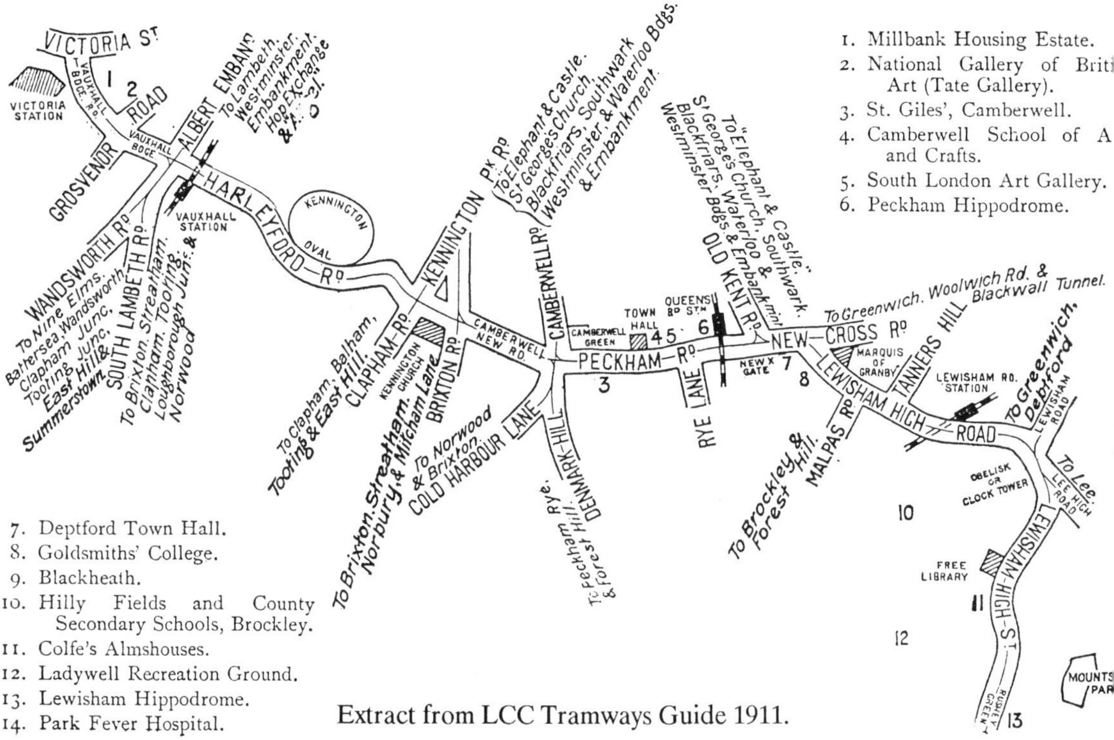

1. Millbank Housing Estate.
2. National Gallery of Briti Art (Tate Gallery).
3. St. Giles', Camberwell.
4. Camberwell School of A and Crafts.
5. South London Art Gallery.
6. Peckham Hippodrome.

7. Deptford Town Hall.
8. Goldsmiths' College.
9. Blackheath.
10. Hilly Fields and County Secondary Schools, Brockley.
11. Colfe's Almshouses.
12. Ladywell Recreation Ground.
13. Lewisham Hippodrome.
14. Park Fever Hospital.

Extract from LCC Tramways Guide 1911.

27. A vital job was done by the pointsmen who worked long hours in all weathers to ensure safety on the tramways. These unsung heroes were hardy souls alert to the hundreds of car movements they had to control. The canvas shelter in this photo gave some protection from the elements; note the point lever being pulled to direct the service 35 tram into Malpas Road. (John H.Meredith)

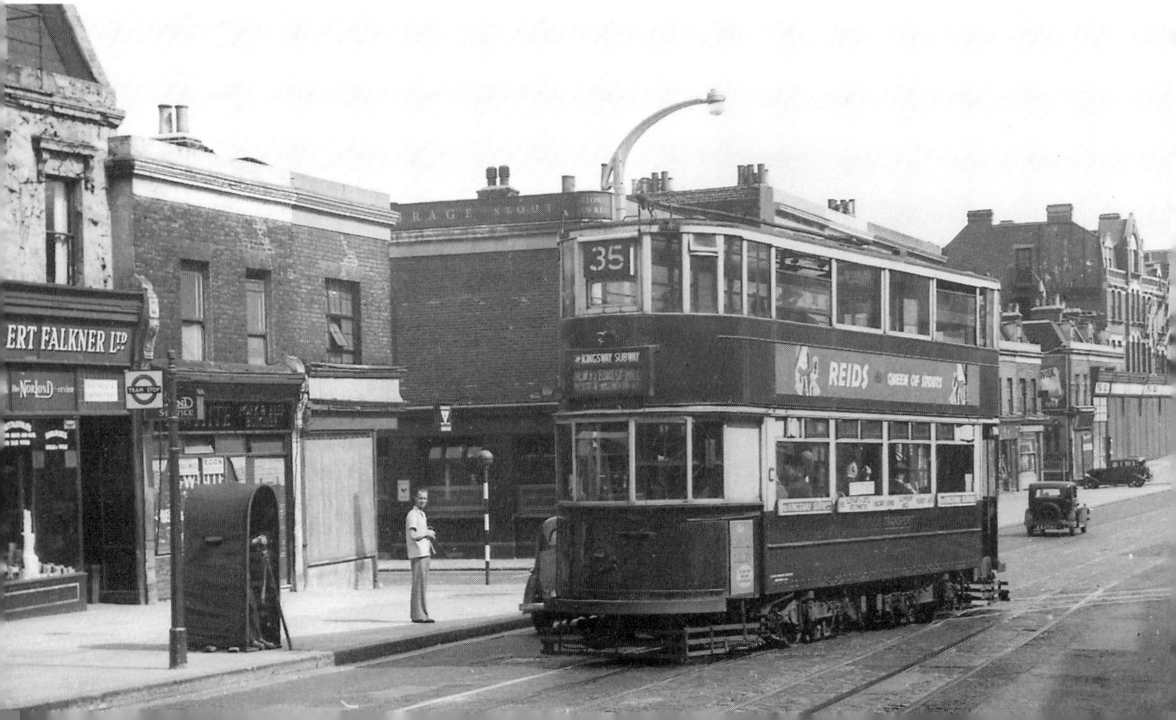

28. Fully laden and Westminster bound an LCC tram glides through St.John's with the spire of the 1855 P.C.Hardwick designed church visible on the left. (R.J.Harley Coll.)

29. St.John's Church overlooks the buildings which served as Lewisham Road station on the Greenwich Park branch. The station was closed in 1917 and is more fully described in the companion Middleton Press volume *Holborn Viaduct to Lewisham*. (R.J.Harley Coll.)

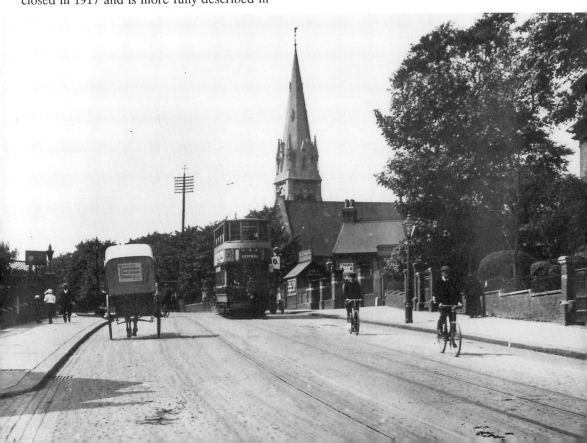

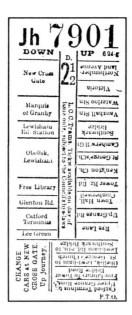

30. Blinding sunshine in S.E.13 as car 1826 ascends the romantically named Loampit Hill. (R.J.S.Wiseman)

31. We reach Lewisham proper and witness the crossing of two forms of electric rail traction. The SR train will be familiar to many readers who have "experienced" rush hour travel in South London. The two gentlemen at the stop are about to board car 1663 outbound to Grove Park. (R.J.S.Wiseman)

32. The vantage point of the railway bridge gives us a view of buildings now swept away in a new road scheme. The tram is crossing the River Ravensbourne at the end of Loampit Vale. Note the fine looking street lamp and the poster advertising the Marlon Brando film at the Rex Cinema. (J.H.Price)

poster advertising the Marlon Brando film at
the Rex Cinema. (J.H.Price)

33. A smile from a carter greets the photographer who has managed to capture the hustle and bustle of pre First World War Lewisham. The conductor of car 131 stands to attention as his vehicle proceeds towards St.Stephen's Church in the background. (J.H.Price Coll.)

34. A group of potential passengers waits patiently for a southbound tram as car 106, later preserved at the National Tramway Museum, loads before setting off for town. (LCC Tramways Trust)

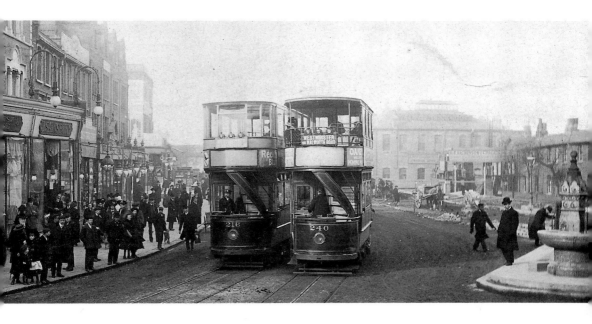

35. Obelisk House, the premises of J.Sainsbury, was the setting every year of a graphic re-enactment of the Boat Race between Oxford and Cambridge. A long chart representing the course would be erected under the shopfront lamps and a marker in the form of a miniature boat of each University would be positioned according to the latest "telephonic" information. (J.H.Price Coll.)

36. The policeman on point duty turns his back on a service 58 tram as it takes the direct road to Greenwich. The roadworks in front of the tram seem suspiciously devoid of workmen, perhaps it was lunch and a "swift half" in the Duke of Cambridge on the corner. A visitor today would be hard put to recognise any of this scene; a ghastly wilderness of tarmac, traffic and roundabout has replaced the buildings. (D.A.Thompson)

3. Lewisham to Blackheath Hill

37. We now follow the lines which climb out of Lewisham towards Blackheath Hill. The tram stop in the shade of the railway bridge was used by numbers of scholars from Colfe's Grammar School which was in temporary accommodation at this time. The whole area had received several direct hits by flying bombs in the latter stages of the war. (D.A.Thompson)

39. On the brow of the hill an RT bus on route 1 puts in an appearance about to overtake Greenwich Borough Council steam roller YM 1496. The latter was right at the edge of its territory on the boundary with Lewisham. Car 1890 takes the climb with ease, seemingly unconcerned with the other road users. (John H.Meredith)

38. Warm spring sunshine greets an encounter between a Royal Arsenal Co-operative Society horse drawn milk float and car 1871 on the single track in Lewisham Road. (D.A.Thompson)

40. A final look at Blackheath Hill and one can almost hear the squeal of the flanges as car 1960 swings into the loop. The companion Middleton Press volume *Greenwich and Dartford Tramways* takes the reader further along this road through to Greenwich. (D.A.Thompson)

4. Lewisham to Lee Green

41. Back at the corner of Lewisham High Street and Loampit Vale, we are now looking south and are just in time to observe a peak hour special on service 36 working from Woolwich to Catford. Service 36 normally ran from Abbey Wood to the Embankment. Sadly the tram on the right has moved out of the camera somewhat. (John H.Meredith)

ROUTE No. 18.
Waterloo Station to Lee Green (Electric Traction).

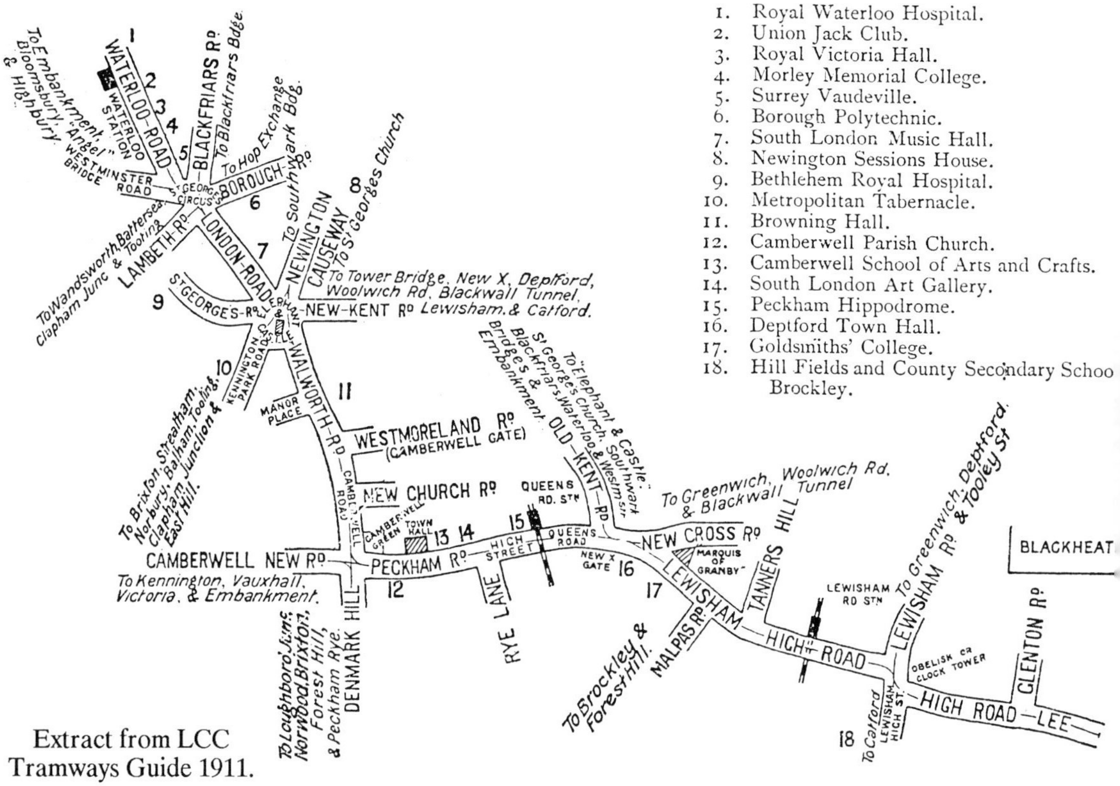

Extract from LCC
Tramways Guide 1911.

1. Royal Waterloo Hospital.
2. Union Jack Club.
3. Royal Victoria Hall.
4. Morley Memorial College.
5. Surrey Vaudeville.
6. Borough Polytechnic.
7. South London Music Hall.
8. Newington Sessions House.
9. Bethlehem Royal Hospital.
10. Metropolitan Tabernacle.
11. Browning Hall.
12. Camberwell Parish Church.
13. Camberwell School of Arts and Crafts.
14. South London Art Gallery.
15. Peckham Hippodrome.
16. Deptford Town Hall.
17. Goldsmiths' College.
18. Hill Fields and County Secondary School, Brockley.

43. The flags are flying over Chiesman's store, perhaps in honour of the Television Demonstrations advertised on the front of the building. An LT inspector glances over from the pointsman's canvas hut; he may be thinking that the 46 tram doesn't belong in the TV age. At any rate it will soldier on for another few months and the inspector, if he owns a television set, will get sore eyes from peering at his nine inch screen! (D.A.Thompson)

←

42. The River Quaggy separates the LCC tramcar from St.Stephen's Church. Notice the three coloured lights above the tram's indicator box; in the era before service numbers these would be illuminated at night to ensure that passengers caught the right tram. This particular car would show green-blue-green on the service from Catford to Westminster. (R.J.Harley Coll.)

45. A gloomy day looking towards Lee High Road and the motorman of car 1390 is no doubt hoping his turn of duty will finish before the fog comes down. At least in a "pea souper" the trams were the only form of road transport to reach their destination without getting lost. (R.J.S.Wiseman)

46. There was a solid quality about Edwardian life and a summer's day long ago reflects the staid world of the shop keepers on Lee High Road. (R.J.Harley Coll.)

47. A taxi halts for a lady to alight from car 1936 outside the Rose of Lee. The new bus stop with its cover is a portent of doom for the tramcar. Soon service 46 will become bus route 182 and the rails with their granite setts will be lifted. (R.J.S.Wiseman)

48. A geography and history lesson by tramcar...to the left of car 113 is the spendid Boone's Chapel built in 1683 by Christopher Boone of Lee Place. Boone was an ancestor of the famous American fontiersman, Daniel Boone. As the tram passes the photographer here outside Newton Parade in Lee High Road, it will cross the Greenwich Meridian and enter the Western Hemisphere. (R.J.Harley Coll.)

49. Crowds turn out to watch car 497 on 25th April 1907 as the Board of Trade inspector checks the line before public service commences. (R.J.Harley Coll.)

50. Car 1979 takes the bend into Lee Green. Could it be that the person who has placed the bike next to the stop has caught the tram to go shopping? In 1951 it was quite easy to indulge in "park and ride" and expect to find your property still there when you returned. (D.A.Thompson)

51 We catch up with the 1907 official inspection again with car 497 posing outside the police station. As one might expect, groups of excited youngsters are avidly following every movement of the new transport wonder. They will then go home and pester the life out of their parents for some coppers for a ride! (J.H.Price Coll.)

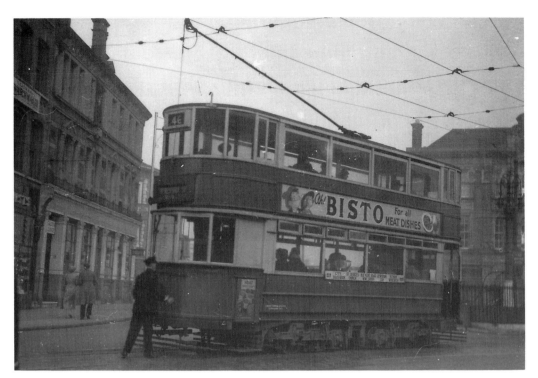

52. The conductor puts up the trolley pole ready for the change over from conduit to overhead at Lee Green. (R.J.S.Wiseman)

53. A car load of tram fans on a very sad day. The chalked inscriptions on this tram at Lee Green change pit have a prophetic quality about them. (John H.Meredith)

5. Lewisham to Grove Park

54. The clock tower at Lewisham is featured in this postcard which was franked 30th May 1907. Everyone seems to be in their Sunday best on this summer evening. (J.H.Price Coll.)

ROUTE 74	Grove Park - New Cross - Elephant & Castle - Blackfriars	P.M. times are in heavy figures

Via Downham Way, Bromley Road, Catford Road, Stanstead Road, Brockley Rise, Stondon Park, Brockley Road, Shardeloes Road (return via Malpas Road), Lewisham Way, New Cross Road, Old Kent Road, London Road, Blackfriars Road, Blackfriars Bridge

RAILWAY STATIONS SERVED: Grove Park, Bellingham, Catford Bridge, Catford, Crofton Park, Brockley, New Cross Gate, Elephant & Castle, Blackfriars

Service interval: MON. to FRI. 6-8 mins., SAT. 5-6 mins. (early morn. 8 mins.), SUN. morn. 12 mins., aft. and eve. 8 mins.

	MON. to FRI. First		MON. to FRI. Last			SATURDAY First		SATURDAY Last		SUNDAY First		SUNDAY Last	
GROVE PARK *Station*		6 38	10 24	11 33		6 38		10 26	11 43		7 42	10 27	11 42
Downham *Change Pit*	6 38	6 47	10 33	11 42	11 46	6 38	6 47	10 35	11 52		7 50	10 36	11 51
Catford *St. Laurence Church*	6 44	6 53	10 39	11 48	11 52	6 44	6 53	10 41	11 58		7 56	10 42	11 57
Cranston Road *Stanstead Road*	6 51	7 0	10 46	11 55	11 59	6 51	7 0	10 48	12 5		8 3	10 49	12 4
Brockley Road *Malpas Road*	7 0	7 9	10 55	12 4	12 8	7 0	7 9	10 57	12 14		8 12	10 58	12 13
New Cross Gate	7 8	7 17	11 3	12 12	12 16	7 8	7 17	11 5	12 22	7 20 / 8 20		11 6	12 21
Old Kent Road *Bricklayers Arms*	7 19	7 28	11 14			7 19	7 28	11 15		7 30 / 8 30		11 16	
Elephant & Castle	7 24	7 33	11 19			7 24	7 33	11 20		7 35 / 8 35		11 21	
BLACKFRIARS *John Carpenter Street*	7 34	7 43	11 28			7 34	7 43	11 28		7 42 / 8 42		11 29	

	MON. to FRI. First		MON. to FRI. Last			SATURDAY First		SATURDAY Last		SUNDAY First		SUNDAY Last	
BLACKFRIARS *John Carpenter Street*		7 35	10 23	10 49	11 30		7 35	10 39	10 51 / 11 30		7 16	10 35	10 51 / 11 3..
Elephant & Castle		7 45	10 32	10 58	11 39		7 45	10 47	10 59 / 11 38		7 23	10 43	10 59 / 11 3..
Old Kent Road *Bricklayers Arms*		7 50	10 37	11 3	11 44		7 50	10 52	11 4 / 11 43		7 28	10 48	11 4 / 11 4..
New Cross Gate	5 54	8 1	10 48	11 14	11 55	5 54	8 1	11 2	11 14 / 11 53	7 0	7 38	10 58	11 14 / 11 5..
Brockley Road *Malpas Road*	6 2	8 9	10 56	11 22		6 2	8 9	11 10	11 22	7 8	7 46	11 6	11 22
Cranston Road *Stanstead Road*	6 11	8 18	11 5	11 31		6 11	8 18	11 19	11 31	7 17	7 55	11 15	11 31
Catford *St. Laurence Church*	6 18	8 25	11 12	11 38		6 18	8 25	11 26	11 38	7 24	8 2	11 22	11 38
Downham *Change Pit*	6 24	8 31	11 18	11 44		6 24	8 31	11 32	11 44	7 30	8 8	11 28	11 45
GROVE PARK *Station*	6 33	8 40	11 27			6 33	8 40	11 41		7 38	8 16	11 37	

EARLIER JOURNEYS—SUNDAY

Catford to Blackfriars at 6 28, 6 44 a.m.
Lewisham *Obelisk* to Savoy Street, via Camberwell Green and Blackfriars at 4 1 a.m.
New Cross to Savoy Street, via Camberwell Green and Westminster at 5 7 a.m.

Savoy Street to New Cross, via Blackfriars and Camberwell Green at 4 39 a.m.
Savoy Street to Catford, via Blackfriars and Camberwell Green at 5 40 a.m.
New Cross to Lewisham *Obelisk* at 3 51 a.m.
New Cross to Catford at 6 2 a.m.

55. A passenger boards from a loading island in front of a pristine looking clock tower which contrasts with the rather grim RACS Tower House. (R.J.S.Wiseman)

56. There aren't many views from horse car days, but here is one looking north along Lewisham High Street. The correspondent has marked the shop where he worked; the card was sent in May 1905. (J.H.Price Coll.)

Extract from 1927 London Travel Guide.

CHEAP FARES by
L.C.C. Tramways

2d. ALL THE WAY.

between Suburban and Central London during the middle hours of the day Monday to Friday (*not* public holidays).

On Cars leaving Central London between **9-30** a.m. and **4-0** p.m. On Cars reaching Central London between **10-30** a.m. and **5** p.m.

In the same period the All-the-way fare for Children under 14 is **1d.** and longer stages are given for the 1d. fare for adults.

5d., 6d., 8d. Return

For Single Fares of **3d., 4d.** and **5d.** respectively.

BOARD THE FIRST CAR.

2d. All-the-way Tickets and (for journeys to or from Central London) Return Tickets are accompanied by transfer facilities.

Whether there is a direct service or not the passenger boards the first car to the change-point and there transfers, if necessary, for the destination required.

These Fares apply to the County of London, Leyton and Wimbledon.

58. St.Mary's Church is the location for a northbound 54 tram as it pulls away from the stop. (Lens of Sutton)

59. Car 1520 passes a 108 bus in Rushey Green. Whilst armed robbery is unfortunately regarded by some villains as a South London speciality, was it really necessary for the two men outside "The Bulldog" to practise the fastest draw in Catford? (John H.Meredith)

61. Catford tramscape as car 1672 waits for car 1874 to reverse. In this photo towards the end of the tramway era the amount of motor traffic competing for road space is beginning to grow. One wonders whether the stairs in the Hovis, Jubilee bread shop had been rendered impassable? (John H.Meredith)

60. At least one top deck passenger eyes the photographer with some curiosity as the motorman shuts off power to coast over the crossover in Rushey Green.
(John H.Meredith)

62. The temporary stop on the pavement indicates that the trams won't be around for much longer in this 5th January 1952 scene, the last day of service 54. (R.J.S.Wiseman)

63. The photographer is standing with his back to the Town Hall; car 102 is about to take the right hand track in the direction of Forest Hill, Camberwell and Victoria. Car 1444 heads the opposite way to reach the same destination, Victoria. No wonder visitors to the capital needed a London Transport tram map to find out where they were going! (John H.Meredith)

64. Time to stand and stare before horse car 878 rolls gently away. The curved track in the foreground leads to the depot.
(R.J.Harley Coll.)

65. The changeover from horse to electric traction was effected in stages. The two forms are seen here with the archway entrance to the horse tram depot in the background. The building was subsequently rebuilt to serve as a garage for Timpson's coaches.
(R.J.Harley Coll.)

ROUTE 62	Lewisham - Forest Hill - Westminster - Savoy Street	P.M. times are in heavy figures

Via Lewisham Road, Lewisham High Street, Rushey Green, Catford Road, Stanstead Road, Park Road, Waldram Road, Devonshire Road, London Road, Lordship Lane, Grove Vale, Dog Kennel Hill, Grove Lane, Champion Park, Denmark Hill, Camberwell Road, Walworth Road, St. Georges Road (return via London Road), Westminster Bridge Road, Westminster Bridge, Victoria Embankment.

RAILWAY STATIONS SERVED : Lewisham, Catford Bridge, Catford, Forest Hill, Lordship Lane, East Dulwich, Denmark Hill, Elephant and Castle, Lambeth North, near Waterloo, Westminster, Charing Cross.

Service interval : MON. to FRI. 12 minutes (peak hours 8 minutes), SAT., morning Forest Hill-Savoy Street 8-10 minutes, afternoon and evening, Lewisham–Elephant and Castle 8-10 mins.

	MONDAY to FRIDAY						SATURDAY							
	First			Last			First			Last				
LEWISHAM ROAD *Lewisham Hill*	..	..	..	...	..	..	...	**3 23**	...	..	...	10 18	10 38	...	..
Lewisham *Clock Tower*	..	..	..	...	..	..	..	**3 25**	...	..	..	10 20	10 40	...	..
Catford *Rushey Green*	..	..	..	...	..	..	..	**3 34**	...	..	..	10 29	10 49	..	..
FOREST HILL *Station*	6 36	..	..	10 15	11 47	..	6 36	**3 43**	...	..	1 53	10 38	10 58	11 47	..
Dulwich *Library*	6 44	..	..	10 23	11 55	...	6 44	**3 51**	...	..	**2 1**	10 46	11 6	11 55	..
Lordship Lane *Goose Green*	6 48	..	..	10 27	11 59	...	6 48	**3 55**	...	..	**2 5**	10 50	11 10	11 59	..
Camberwell Green	6 58	..	..	10 37	**12 9**	...	6 58	**4 5**	...	..	**2 15**	11 0	11 20	**12 9**	..
Elephant & Castle	7 8	..	..	10 47	..	...	7 8	**4 15**	..	..	**2 25**	11 10	..	..	..
EMBANKMENT *Savoy Street*	7 20	..	..	10 59	..	..	7 20	..	...	..	**2 38**	....	..	...	..
EMBANKMENT *Savoy Street*	..	7 21	..	11 0	..	....	..	7 21	...	..	**2 39**	....	..	...	..
Elephant & Castle	..	7 33	..	11 12	..	..	..	7 33	**2 33**	..	**2 52**	9 44	11 12	..	..
Camberwell Green	6 11	7 43	..	11 22	..	....	6 11	7 43	**2 37**	**2 43**	**3 2**	9 54	11 22	..	..
Lordship Lane *Goose Green*	6 21	7 53	..	11 32	..	..	6 21	7 53	**2 47**	**2 53**	**3 12**	10 4	11 32	..	..
Dulwich *Library*	6 25	7 57	..	11 36	..	..	6 25	7 57	**2 51**	**2 57**	**3 16**	10 8	11 36	..	..
FOREST HILL *Station*	6 33	8 5	..	11 44	..	..	6 33	8 5	**2 59**	**3 5**	**3 24**	10 16	11 44	..	..
Catford *Rushey Green*	..	..	..	..	..	..	..	..	**3 8**	**3 14**	..	10 25	..	..	..
Lewisham *Clock Tower*	..	..	..	..	..	..	..	..	**3 17**	**3 23**	..	10 34	..	..	..
LEWISHAM ROAD *Lewisham Hill*	..	..	..	..	..	..	..	..	**3 19**	**3 25**	..	10 36	..	..	..

66. Lewisham Town Hall is somewhat obscured by liberal amounts of public transport. (John H.Meredith)

MD 9832

DOWN	D.	UP
Grosvenor Road	1	Victoria
Vauxhall Station	2	Grosvenor Road
Kennington Church		Vauxhall Station
Camberwell Green		Kennington Church
Town Hall Camberwell		Camberwell Green
Rye Lane		Town Hall Camberwell
Queen's Rd. Station		Rye Lane
New Cross Gate		Queen's Rd. Station
Marquis of Granby		New Cross Gate
Tanner's Hill		Marquis of Granby
Lewisham Rd. Station		Tanner's Hill
Goslax Lewisham		Lewisham Rd. Station
Lewisham Public Liby.		Lewisham
Wlenton Rd.		Lewisham Public Liby.
Catford		Wlenton Road
Lee Green		Catford

67. Car 1025 achieved fame by being saved from the scrap heap; it is now an exhibit at the LT Museum in Covent Garden. In November 1951, still hard at work, it was captured here on film doing its best to race past the opposition assembled on the forecourt of Catford bus garage. (John H.Meredith)

68. Most of the windows and the front bulkhead door to the driver are open on a hot day in Bromley Road, Bellingham, in August 1949. (John H.Meredith)

69. Where Allerford Road joins Bromley Road the stately procession of tramcars continues giving the public an unrivalled service from home to shops or work. (John H.Meredith)

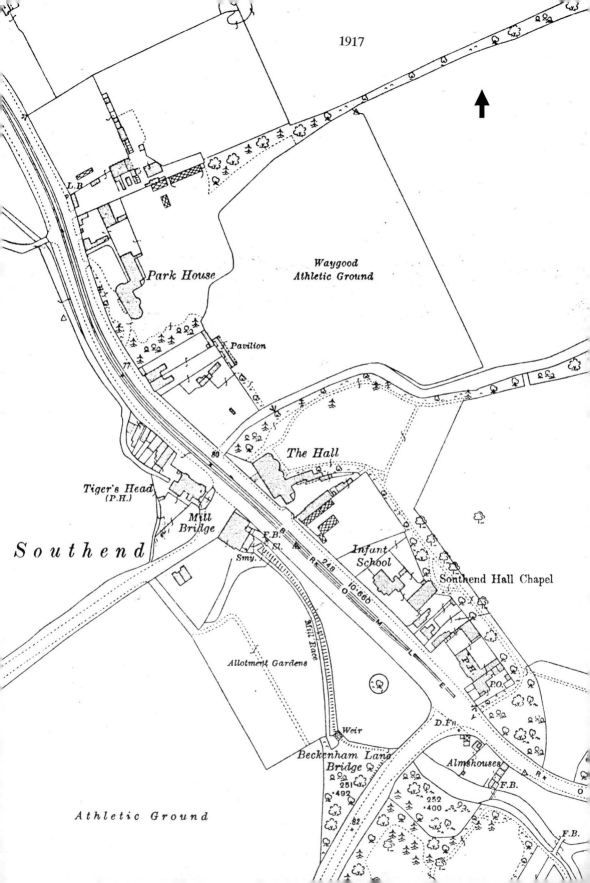

70. At Southend Village terminus in the early
1920s; car 45 dates from 1903 and is beginning
to show its age, whereas car 1651 of 1911 shows
less body sag. (D.A.Thompson Coll.)

←

71. The LCC tramways reached Southend Village in April 1914 and the car by the gas lamp is about to enter the terminal stub. (J.H.Price Coll.)

←

72. Still retaining something of a rural atmosphere, the Southend area of the Metropolitan Borough of Lewisham is the setting for three trams all with different indicator boxes and service number displays. (D.A.Thompson)

73. Car 2047 started its career in Walthamstow, Essex before its compulsory acquisition by LT and subsequent transfer south of the river. Always known as speedy cars, one overtakes a van at Southend Village crossover on Bromley Road. Another Green Line coach can be glimpsed to the front of the tram. (John H.Meredith)

UNDERTAKERS
54
NEW CROSS GATE
FRANCIS J. PEEL & SONS
KELLOW
FASHIONWEAR
COSTUMIER
MILLINERY
T. HARRIS

PROSECUTED

74. Turning out of Downham Way, car 1784 has no trouble with other traffic, only a couple of bicycles and the odd pedestrian are about on this sleepy summer day. The residents here were used to the sound of tramcars during the sleeping hours as LT all night tram route 5 used to terminate at Downham. (D.A.Thompson)

75. The grand rehousing plan developed by the LCC in the 1920s consisted of new estates, some like the one at Downham, served by tramway extensions. Local children play at the rail head; soon workmen will arrive to lay more tracks through the countryside.
(LCC Tramways Trust)

76. The fields have now been covered by houses and a change pit has been installed at the beginning of Downham Way. A characteristic moment on London's tramways is witnessed here as a crew member swings the pole to stow it under the hook on the car roof. (John H.Meredith)

77. Looking westwards from Downham change pit, we meet car 2 again still gleaming bright in its smart LT red and cream livery. The trolley is on the wire and the car is about to move forward drawing power from the overhead after having ejected its plough where the two gentlemen are standing. It was a matter of pride in days gone by that public service vehicles went out on the road regularly cleaned. (D.A.Thompson)

78. The extension to Valeswood Road crossover was opened in September 1926; car 962 is pictured about this time with its trolley already positioned for the return to London. As the scene suggests, the number of passengers was limited to building workers and the occasional tripper who wanted to ride to the end of the line. (LCC Tramways Trust)

79. A quarter of a century later at the same spot as the previous photo, another reversal takes place, though this time the track goes on to Grove Park. (D.A.Thompson)

80. In April 1933 the LCC conducted experiments with new current collectors. Here car 1172 halts in Downham Way sporting a pantograph instead of the conventional trolley pole. As it was, the tests were inconclusive; most tramway research and development ceased with the coming of London Transport in July 1933. (National Tramway Museum)

81. Contributors to the Tramway Classics series include Don Thompson who made the journey from his North London home to record the declining tramway scene. He maintains that he often set off under bright sunshine only to find that it was raining in South London! He seems to have had better luck here as car 2 picks up on Downham Way. (D.A.Thompson)

82. "Putting on the anchors" was tramway talk for using the brakes. Car 1498 approaches Southover crossover with the motorman pumping sand on the tracks to assist adhesion as he pulls to a halt. Hence the dust seen rising from the rails. (John H.Meredith)

83. Journey's end, the terminus at Grove Park. Car 1310 reverses to load folk out shopping on this August day in 1949. The shelter, the tram stop and the fashions of the period all add interest to the scene. (John H.Meredith)

84. In the opposite direction to the previous photo, car 1628 waits its turn. The technically minded reader may have noticed that standard trolleybus overhead fittings were used at Grove Park. Whether this was done as a preliminary to the pre-war conversion programme, we do not know; in the event trolleybuses never reached this location. Service 74 was replaced by diesel buses in January 1952, and a new bus station was opened on the other side of the railway. (D.A.Thompson)

X 3629

TO 25B L.C.C. Trams TO

17	Beckenham Lane	Ser. 54	Victoria	1
16	Bellingham Rd		Regency Street	2
15	St. Laurence Church Catford		Vauxhall	3
			Church	4
14	Lewisham Public Library		Vassall Road	5
13	Obelisk Lewisham		Camberwell Green	6
12	Lewisham Rd. Stn.		Camberwell Town Hall	7
11	Marquis of Granby or Malpas Road		Rye Lane	8
10	New Cross Gate		Queen's Road Stn.	9

LU 3296

DOWN AND RANSFER

Available for transfer to another car at New X Gate only

Lewisham Road Station to Old Kent Road Station

	D. 1	
Kennington Church		Victoria
Camberwell Green		Vauxhall Station
Rye Lane		Kennington Church
Queen's Road Station		Camberwell Green
New Cross Gate		Town Hall Camberwell
Marquis of Granby		Rye Lane
Lewisham Road Station		Queen's Road Station
Obelisk, Lewisham		New Cross Gate
Catford		Lewisham Rd.
Lee Green		

When punched below the double black line, this ticket is available only on car on which issued.

Uo 0883

TO 25B L.C.C. Trams

17	Beckenham Lane	Ser. 54	Victoria	1
16	Bellingham Rd		Regency Street	2
15	St. Laurence Church Catford		Vauxhall	3
			Church	4
14	Lewisham Public Library		Vassall Road	5
13	Obelisk Lewisham		Camberwell Green	6
12	Lewisham Rd. Stn.		Camberwell Town Hall	7
11	Marquis of Granby or Malpas Road		Rye Lane	8
10	New Cross Gate		Queen's Road Stn.	9

6. Catford to Forest Hill

85. Car 145 stands in the midst of an array of period street furniture; it is easy to forget how streets looked before yellow lines and plastic traffic bollards. Behind the No Waiting sign and the tram stop is the entrance to Lewisham Town Hall at Rushey Green. (R.J.S.Wiseman)

86. A lady wheels her bicycle by the kerb as car 1678 accelerates up the grade at Catford Bridge. The date on the back of this postcard is given as July 1921. (R.J.Harley Coll.)

Extract from 1927 London Travel Guide.

87. Most transport museums would now go to great lengths to acquire the vehicles which have come together by chance in this shot of Catford Bridge. Car 562 is pursued by a Lewisham dust cart which has just nosed ahead of an RTL bus. (Lens of Sutton)

88. The railway from Catford station crosses Catford Hill with car 109 about to pass a motor cycle and sidecar. The gentleman in the tailored jacket who is walking along the pavement seems to be having some trouble with a child's folding pushchair.
(D.A.Thompson)

89. The air of suburban peace and tranquility in Stanstead Road is only touched by the noise of the tram approaching the crossover by Beechfield Road. (D.A.Thompson)

90. An inspector can just be seen using the telephone on the section box at the junction of Stanstead Road and Brockley Rise. On the green light car 1986 will turn left past the Invicta Laundry. (John H.Meredith)

←

91. There is evidence of bomb damage behind car 1908 as it negotiates the sharp bend from Stanstead Road into Sunderland Road. Tramways have the advantage over conventional railways in that they can take severe curves and steep gradients in their stride. (D.A.Thompson)

93. Waldram Park Road, Waldram Crescent junction, Forest Hill and the last passenger gets off before the terminus. (John H.Meredith)

←

92. A hundred yards on from the previous view, car 132 has just left Waldram Park Road. Some of the property to the right of the tram had seen better days. (D.A.Thompson)

94. The author remembers a holiday poster from his childhood which featured a line of ducks crossing the tram tracks in Copenhagen. Forest Hill came somewhat lower down the scale of our feathered friends and could only manage a rather scruffy quartet of pigeons ambling across the entrance to Perry Vale. (D.A.Thompson)

95. The terminus at Forest Hill was laid out as a lay-by from the main line in Waldram Park Road. Here car 1980 waits with storm clouds gathering over Lewisham. (D.A.Thompson)

96. A final look at the Perry Vale terminus and car 153 which is ahead of schedule has nipped into the siding after the conductor has pulled the point lever in the foreground.
(John H.Meredith)

Steady...!
BLACKPOOL
its a vintage beer...
BASS
RED TRIANGLE
R·A·F
NATIONAL
Savings Certificates
3
Buy all you can
SOUTHE
FORES
LONDON in 12
Have a
CAPSTAN
REIDS
QUEEN OF STOUTS
Bourn-vita
By GAS thats lovely!

58
VICTORIA via DULWICH
PJ
WALLER
LTD.
OFFICES & STORES

97. In order to reach the Dulwich lines the trams had to pass under the railway at Forest Hill. One can see quite clearly where the highway has been lowered under the bridge to accommodate double deck tramcars. (D.A.Thompson)

98. The pawnbroker's shop in Devonshire Road is passed by a tram, the noise of traction motors straining up the hill was a familiar sound at this location. (D.A.Thompson)

99. The former clock tower at Forest Hill station stands sentinel as car 106 coasts round the corner. The story of this station is told in the *London Bridge to East Croydon* railway album. (D.A.Thompson)

7. Brockley to New Cross

100. At the foot of Brockley Rise the pointwork
leading to Stanstead Road can be observed.
(R.J.S.Wiseman)

101. The corner of Brockley Rise and Stondon
Park is the setting for car 169. A minor detail
is that this tram has its trolley poles crossed and
fixed to the opposite retaining hooks on the
roof. (John H.Meredith)

102. A motor cyclist emerges from Honor Oak Park as car 1844 waits at the stop on this August day in 1951. Author, musician and comedian Spike Milligan lived for some years in Riseldine Road just out of camera shot. Local tram journeys make several appearances in his writings and he must have known this stop well. (R.J.S.Wiseman)

1911 advert.

103. In Brockley Road by Sevenoaks Road we witness a cameo of life in 1951. The stacking of setts for track repairs has forced a disabled gentleman in a wheelchair on to the roadway. Note that he is collecting for charity; a schoolboy smartly attired in regulation socks, short trousers, blazer, tie and cap peers at the photographer. (John H.Meredith)

104. We now arrive at the hump back bridge at Crofton Park station. The railway did not open here until 1892 (see the album *Crystal Palace (High Level) and Catford Loop*) and so had only a brief monopoly before the advent of electric trams in 1913. (D.A.Thompson)

ROUTE No. 19. Southwark Bridge to Forest Hill (Waldram Road) and Catford, and Greenwich to Catford (Electric Traction).

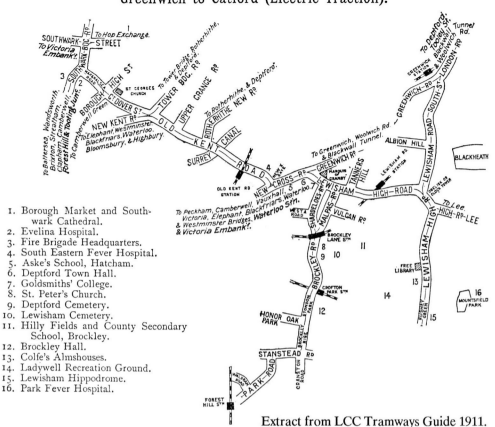

Extract from LCC Tramways Guide 1911.

1. Borough Market and Southwark Cathedral.
2. Evelina Hospital.
3. Fire Brigade Headquarters.
4. South Eastern Fever Hospital.
5. Aske's School, Hatcham.
6. Deptford Town Hall.
7. Goldsmiths' College.
8. St. Peter's Church.
9. Deptford Cemetery.
10. Lewisham Cemetery.
11. Hilly Fields and County Secondary School, Brockley.
12. Brockley Hall.
13. Colfe's Almshouses.
14. Ladywell Recreation Ground.
15. Lewisham Hippodrome.
16. Park Fever Hospital.

105. Car 183 is caught about to traverse the crossover to the north of Crofton Park station. A diminutive delivery truck, EKR 805, has just unloaded supplies to the nearby shops. (John H.Meredith)

106. A view dating from 1911 shows car 273 under the railway bridge at Brockley Lane station which had the unfortunate distinction of being shut down completely in 1917. It was on the Greenwich Park branch. (R.J.Harley Coll.)

107. At the parting of the ways a 35 tram prepares to take the London bound track along Shardeloes Road. The "down" line was in the adjacent Malpas Road. This one way arrangement is known to the tramway fraternity as "Cannon Hilling" after a similar method used in Birmingham. (D.A.Thompson)

108. Malpas Road near Brockley Cross sees car 994 swaying happily through the suburban scene with Bob the greengrocer displaying his wares. The delivery bike is parked outside for that extra personal service. (John H.Meredith)

109. A final look at Malpas Road with its small corner shops and postbox. Perhaps the lad staring at the tram grew up to be an enthusiast? (D.A.Thompson)

110. Solid rows of terrace houses are only broken by a post-war block of flats here in Shardeloes Road. Car 1977 heads north towards New Cross and central London. (D.A.Thompson)

111. We say "Farewell" in a literal sense with this last photo of our nostalgic journey. In a few hours service 35 will be no more and the track in Shardeloes Road will fall silent for all time. Motorman and conductor pose, both looking somewhat uncertain at the prospect of a diesel bus future. (R.J.S.Wiseman)

8. Rolling Stock E1 class

112. An official builder's photo taken in 1921 of car 1727. Note the striking LCC livery of purple lake and cream with gold lining. Trucks and undergear were painted red oxide. The truck mounted plough carrier can clearly be seen. (National Tramway Museum. Hurst, Nelson)

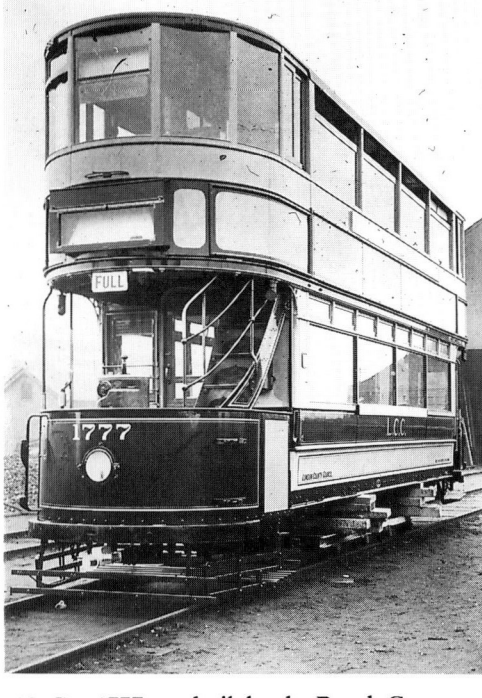

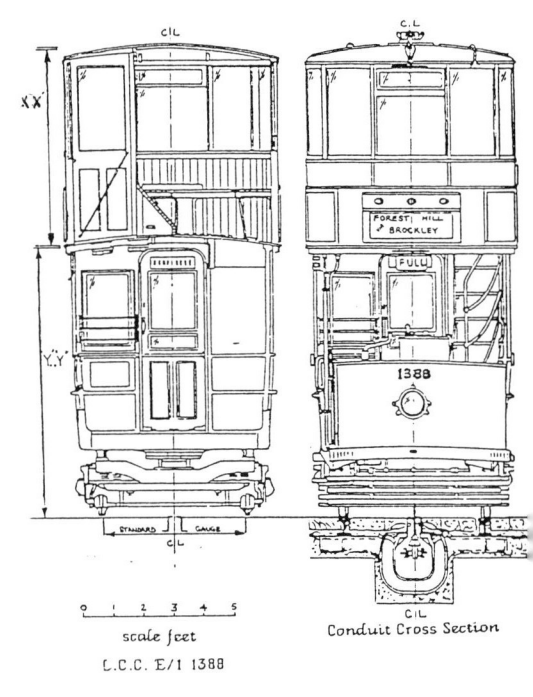

113. Car 1777 was built by the Brush Company of Loughborough. It is seen here having been wheeled out on temporary trucks for the photo call. The fittings on the dash and the drawbar coupling indicate that this tram was destined to take part in the LCC trailer experiment. (National Tramway Museum. Brush)

114. Pictured in 1948 just after a repaint, car 1613 is resplendent in LT red and cream with gold/yellow lining. The trucks are now painted black and the plough carrier has been repositioned centrally, attached to the car body and not to the truck. (D.A.Thompson)

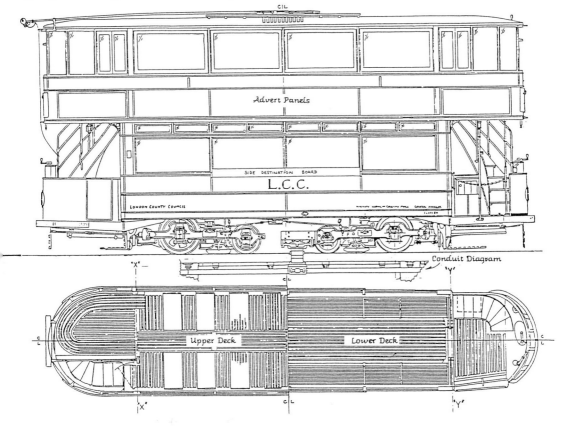

Advert Panels

SIDE DESTINATION BOARD

L.C.C.

LONDON COUNTY COUNCIL

Conduit Diagram

Upper Deck

Lower Deck

Class E/1 cars formed the backbone of the LCC fleet and the first batch was ordered from Hurst, Nelson in 1907. Basically this type of tram represented all that was "tried and tested" in the LCC experience of supplying a reliable tramway service to Londoners. Cars 752-1676 were delivered before the First World War with cars 1727-1851 following from 1921. Apart from some early cars, all trams in these batches came with trolley poles so that they could be used in the outer suburbs and on joint services with other company and municipal systems. In the mid 1920s a "Pullmanisation" programme was carried out to upgrade the E/1s; transverse seats were fitted to the lower deck of each tram and other improvements were made to enhance passenger comfort.

London Transport made a half-hearted attempt at tramway modernisation in the mid and late 1930s when around 150 E/1s were subjected to rehabilitation, which amounted to a partial rebuild of each car with windscreens, new flush sides, new seats and internal improvements. These cars were known to enthusiasts as the "rehabs" and the LCC Tramways Trust is currently restoring car 1622 to rehab. condition so that it can take its place amongst the fleet at the National Tramway Museum.

The original LCC livery colours were described as purple lake and primrose; the lake colour weathered over the years to a dark brown. In the mid-1920s a new, brighter livery of crimson and cream appeared; the gold LCC initials on the waist panel were replaced by the LCC coat of arms.

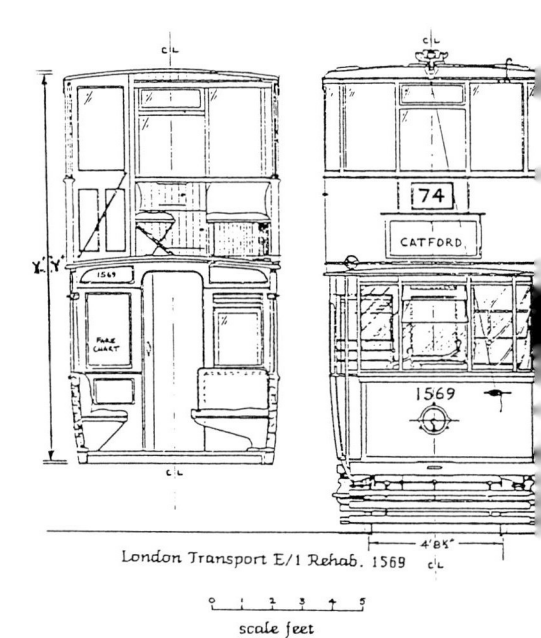

London Transport E/1 Rehab. 1569

scale feet

115. The top deck of a standard E/1. When the weather was cold it was a draughty place to sit and the author's father used to maintain that the chap who invented frozen fish fingers got the idea from watching numbed top deck passengers in the artic winter of 1947! (D.A.Thompson)

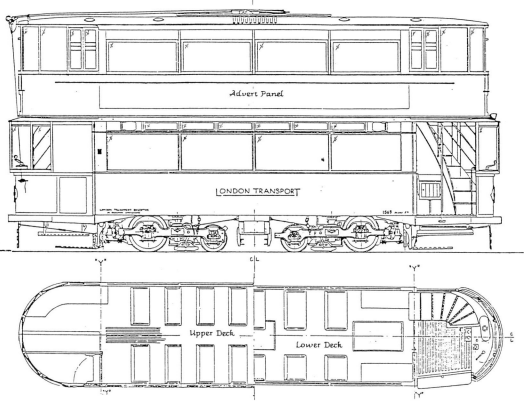

116. The lower deck of car 1530 looks quite cosy with the bulkhead door closed. The glazed panels at the bulkhead were tinted so as not to reflect the glare of the lower saloon lights on the driver's windscreen. (D.Jones Coll.)

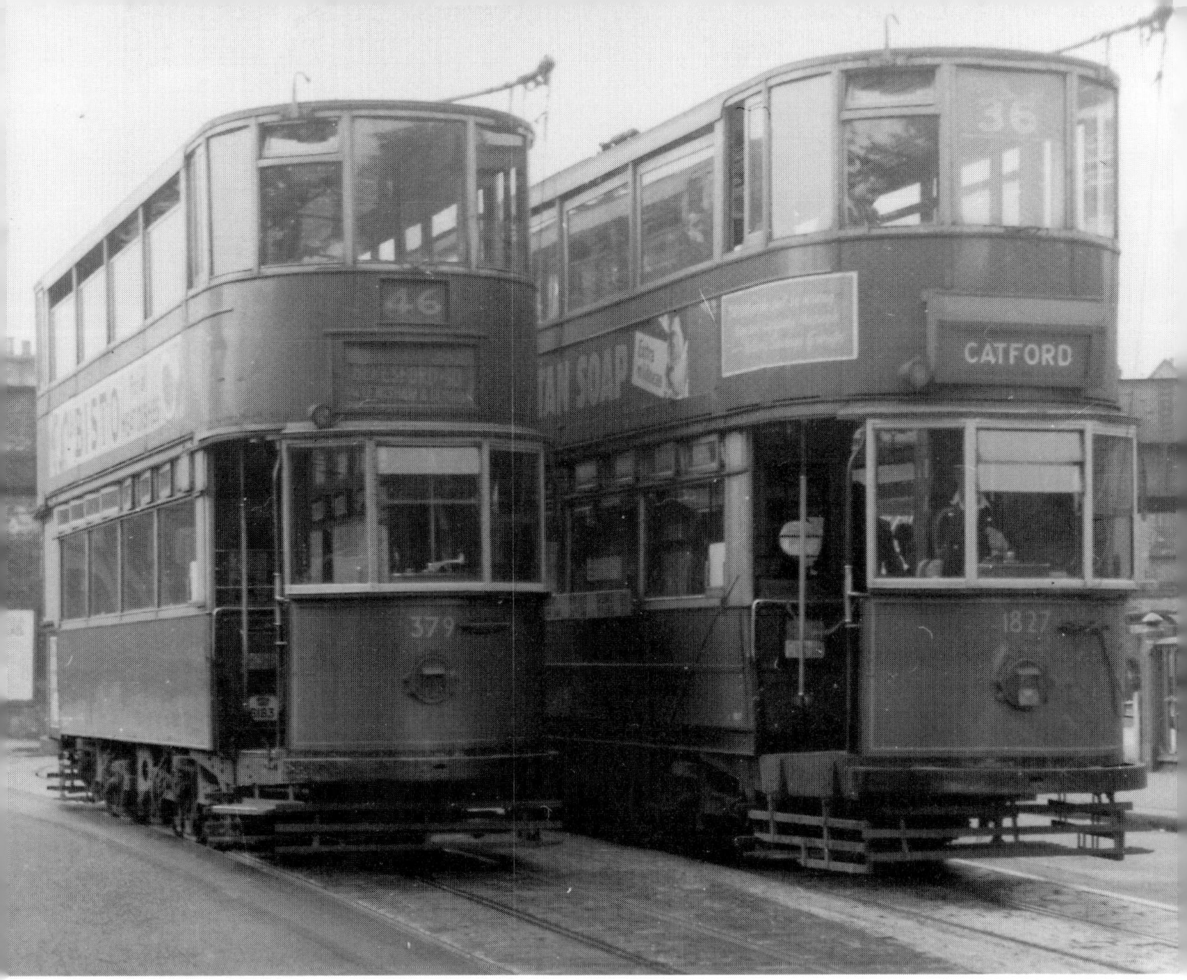
46
CATFORD
36
TAN SOAP
379
1827

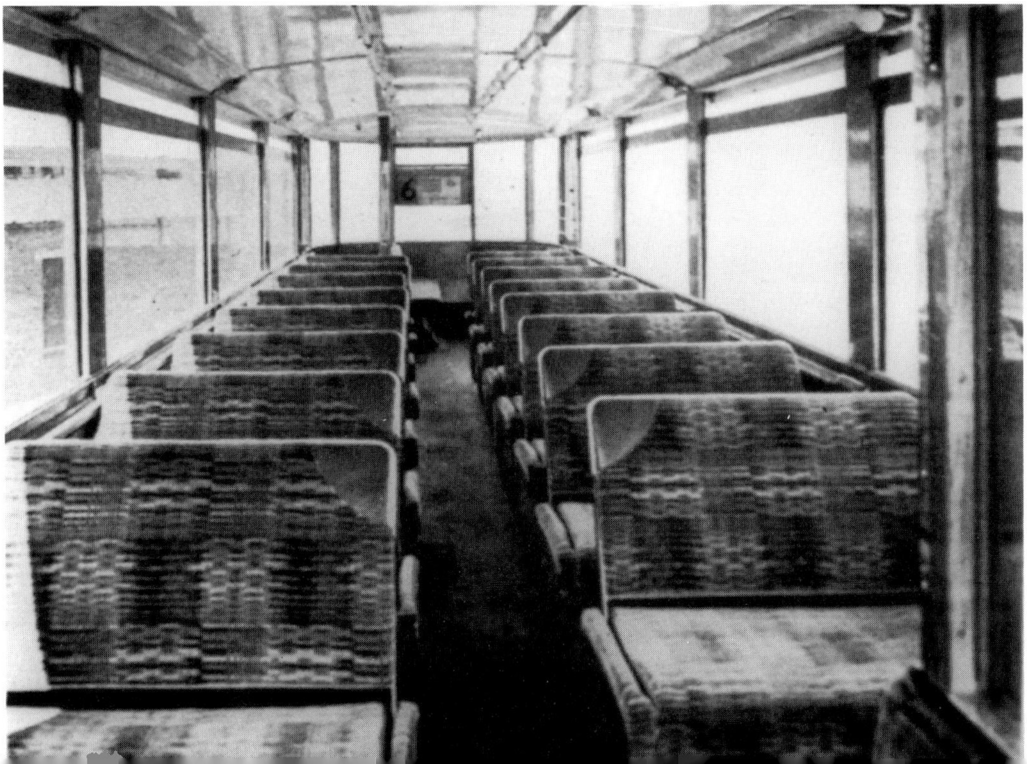

119. The "business end" of an E/1 tramcar. This is known as a maximum traction truck and there were two under each car; the motor was rated at around 60 horse power. Track gauge was standard and also visible here between the two wheels is the magnetic track brake. (D.A.Thompson)

117. Both cars pictured here in summer 1951 were coming to the end of their active lives. They illustrate some of the differences between rehab. 379 and the LT standard E/1 car 1827. In fact car 379 is an impostor as it hails originally from Croydon Corporation, but for the puposes of this exercise it can be regarded as a typical example of an LT rehabilitated tram. (John H.Meredith)

118. The upper deck of rehab. car 1038 had been furnished with new "sandy-green" coloured moquette covered seats and chromium light fittings. (D.Jones Coll.)

120. A pleasing sight to end this album is this view of car 1622 under reconstruction by the LCC Tramways Trust. Many hours of volunteer labour and specialist help have gone into the project and it is hoped that the result will be seen running soon at the National Tramway Museum in Crich, Derbyshire. (D.Jones)